BERYL THE FERAL

@micktheclick

Blessed with the misfortune being a rebel who loves rules, a chronic introvert who deeply people; Beryl the Feral is an insatiable Playsmith and *felice*-ilitator, who lives to encourage authentic expression. A list-making, rule-breaking emotional percolator, who tends to think too much and care too deeply about more things than are generally convenient.

When she is not hiding in her caravan, Beryl can mostly be found wandering the South West with her trusty backpack, bringing ragged elegance and wild intelligence to a variety of endeavours enabling others' creativity. These include her own spoken-word festival stage and 'performance poetry on prescription' workshops for the NHS (see the back of the book for more details).

Aspiring to inspire, Beryl is a champion for self-awareness, truth and validation, welcoming the mangled imperfections of being alive with as much wonder as she can muster. As a highly animated performer, her on-stage accolades include appearances at Ways With Words, WOMAD, and the Whitstable Biennale, as well as being a founder member of the Wondermentalist Cabaret and co-creator of a series of interactive poetry gameshows.

Beryl has previously appeared in print in a variety of anthologies and periodicals, including books by Bloomsbury and Transition Towns, as well as selling many copies of her popular self-published collections.

Besides deep connection with people, she loves small things, stories, games, dressing-up, playfighting and loads of other stuff (which you'll find out as you read).

And she especially loves it when you buy her book.

My Other Poems Are Funnier

Beryl the Feral

Burning Eye

BurningEyeBooks
Never Knowingly
Mainstream

This edition published by Burning Eye Books 2018

www.burningeye.co.uk

@burningeyebooks

Burning Eye Books
15 West Hill, Portishead, BS20 6LG

ISBN 978-1-911570-36-3

My Other Poems
Are Funnier

Acknowledgements

You rock

may I be patient
with the safety and evasion
necessary in the small-talk walking
beside every fleeting guest.
But God bless the merciless truth
in which I can rest.

CONTENTS

Introduction 12

GLIDING
INSPIRED BY RYALLS PARK POETRY POSSE '18 16
ALIEN LAMENT 17
PLENTY IDENTITIES 18
ATTENTION WHORE 20
I WOZ ERE 22
TO DO (OR FIRST WORLD PROBLEMS) 23

SLIDING
PRIORITIES 28
RESENTFULLY YOURS 29
NO 30
FREQUENT FREQUENCIES 31
GOOD MORNING 32
LET THEM EAT... 33

COLLIDING
I'M SUCH AN OXYMORON SOMETIMES 38
KNIGHT WITH THE DOUBLE-EDGED SWORD 40
PHONE CALL 42

COPING
SCIENCE-FICTION FANTASY 46
UPSIDE 48
IRRATIONAL PASSION 49
BAD DAY 50
I DECLINE 51

MOPING
SEEMING UNSEEN 54
ALTARED 55
LOW POINT 56
THE FALL 57

HOPING

THE SKIN I WAS IN   60
SOMETHING ABOUT A CAMEL AND A NEEDLE   61
SHAMEAWAY   64
SORRY   66
RAVEN IMAGE   67

CLIMBING

INSPIRED BY RYALLS PARK POETRY POSSE '17   72
OVER YOULOGY   74
FOR JEFF (AND EVERYONE EVER)   75

SHINING

I LIKE ME   80
REASONS TO BE CHEERFUL   81
AFFIRMATION SONG!   83

OWNING IT

BELIEVE THE BIRD   86
IN MY DEFENCE   87
SMALL PRINT   88
HYPERGRAPHIA   90
BLOOMIN' HARD WORK   92
WOMANIFESTO   93
IN THE MOMENT   94

About the Word/Play Project   97

INTRODUCTION

A book is a strange kind of kudos, which despite looking and sounding impressively professional is really no more significant or meaningful than the work I do running workshops, performing, or distributing my handmade zines...

But my hope is that with, and through, Burning Eye's incredible endorsement, the reach of this book might be further and so touch someone or even change a life that it otherwise wouldn't.

It's for that reason that this is not a disparate showcase of my best or cleverest poems (though it does include some old favourites), but instead is a collection on the theme of radical honesty, self-inquiry and mental health.

In fact it's a beautiful kind of irony that someone whose self-esteem evaporates so easily off the bathroom mirror should receive such a validation as being published when her particular submission happens to be all about exposing imperfections. Go figure.

If you're the sort of unique being that reads a poetry book cover to cover in sequence, you might notice in here a vague trip around the inner wheel of dissolution and restoration. I'm personally dizzy from riding this heroic carousel so many times, but I wouldn't give it up - and I offer this token companion for anyone in the same tumultuous folds of stripping away untruths and deeply meeting themselves, in the hope that we can all eventually befriend our own remarkable oddness.

My poems are usually made with performance in mind, and tend to evolve as they are spoken. It's a big thing to concretise any snapshot moment of time in print, and there are countless other themes, poems and even words I could have selected for inclusion. But for now, my work is to surrender this as a well-intentioned and Good Enough offering (yes, even though some bits aren't deep or funny and still make me squirm with their blatancy). As I would tell any other writer, the importantest thing is to share and be welcome.

(As performance poets we are always told we should never apologise before presenting our work. But what is a book about self-esteem without a bashful disclaimer? And yes, I know 'importantest' isn't a word. But it is what I would say.)

BtF

GLIDING

INSPIRED BY RYALLS PARK POETRY POSSE '18

Every person has a story,
and every story must be told.
And every truth deserves its time,
and every heart a hand to hold.

Each determined in the darkness
is a soldier of the soul,
every scarring is a medal,
every wounded man is whole.

Every child inside should have its comfort,
every tear not fear to flow,
every loss not be borne alone,
and every greatness get to grow,

every small success be celebrated,
every miracle be awed.
Every person has a story -
I'll tell you mine, you tell me yours...

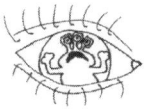

ALIEN
LAMENT

I'm a pink and flubby alien behind an eyeball screen,
in a giant body spaceship that's a human-life machine.
And I don't know how I got here,
and I don't know how to drive,
so it's been a bloody miracle to keep this thing alive!
'Cause there aren't any instructions - and it doesn't seem to slow;
in fact, if there's a brake somewhere I'd really like to know,
because the hands and mouth just do things
and the world keeps passing by,
and no one sees this frantic pilot waving from the eye...
and asteroids are bouncing off the bonnet all the while,
and I'm swerving for survival while I just operate the smile,
and this spaceship's screaming onwards
with sparks flying in its wake,
and there's no emergency cord and no glass that I can break.
And the dial on the desk is going red, it's going to pop,
and I don't know how to work it
and I don't know how to stop,
'cause I'm just a flubby alien. I come from outer space!
And now I've wound up in a body,
somehow trapped behind this face.
And all the other bodies out there, like you and you and you...
you all seem so together, but are you flubby inside, too?

PLENTY IDENTITIES

These are the "mes" I would like you to meet.
I will introduce my egos in their character conceit.
We exist together pleasantly, each holds an equal place,
but who knows which is here right now
and looking through this face...?

There's the one who wears the outfit with the 'B' upon her chest;
she's everyone's favourite, does everything best.
She doesn't ever make mistakes, or feel any pain;
she's no place for insecurity, or doubt or fear or shame.

That one who's always carrying round a concrete block,
wearing dirty dungarees and a patent pair of Docs -
she is strong, a survivor, she always comes through.
She can dig, she can lift things, and she doesn't need you.

The one in all the black clothes who is covering her face,
who is standing in the background, won't impose upon the space;
she is low-key and tiptoes, she hardly dares breathe;
she is grateful, and takes up much less than she needs.

And looking up with large eyes and a practised little pout
is the one who needs you to sort everything out.
She is dizzy and clumsy, forgetful and shy,
but don't slip up and defy her 'cause she's guaranteed to cry!

The one with ample bosom and the wide open arms,
who gives dozens of cuddles, who comforts and calms:
she will listen without judgment, she will soothe out all your woe,
she doesn't have a single thing that others need to know.

The one in the all-rainbow clothes, the hair dye and the wings,
who jumps around in somersaults and shouts out loud and sings:
She is queer, she is crazy, she is often undressed,
she is ne'er perturbed by any dare - don't put it to the test!

There's a dirty stinky pleb in me who neglects to have a wash.
She delights in provocation, and she couldn't give a toss.
She's hairy and she's lairy and she doesn't care for rules;
you'll be left alone with your concerns like poor misguided fools.

And somewhere there's a teacher, who looks down her nose at
    you.
And anything that you've done, you can bet she's done it too.
She is tight with information, she can make you feel quite small,
but beware if she is watching you and doesn't speak at all...

But the one of me who's lonely, and terrified, and weak:
we voted her out years ago, she isn't here to speak.
She's hurting and she's ugly and she wounded and she's plain.
But we sent someone to look for her - she may show up again...

ATTENTION WHORE

I'm an attention whore; I always need more.
I live to be loved,
Suckling the blood of admirers; look at me.
Adored/awed/never ignored,
must be special,
cannot be average/taken for granted/alone.

I will lap up your love like a princess on fire
if I know you're growing and I'm your desire.
Clear those ideas which tire and distract,
watch only my eyes; see they're not downcast.
Wipe the landscape from your mind,
dress my wounds/dry my eyes,
put your hand on my thigh when we're driving
and guide me with a palm on the small of my back
in the street, reach out each time I feel lonely,
sing to me/read/write poetry,
look at my skin hungrily,
touch me, touch me, touch me.

Rub my shoulders, watch my moods alter,
see when I falter,
keep all my letters and build me an altar,
call me each night, come around uninvited,
tightly squeeze my knee beneath family display,
beg me to stay/hang on every word I say,

pursue my silent trails/send me mail,
bring me gifts/take me when you can't resist,
ease my clit as it aches when I wake.
Kiss me while I'm sleeping,
and the world will be safe.

I'm an attention whore, always need more.
I live to be loved; look at me. (Could it be
I'm insecure?)

I WOz ERE

Gaily skipping through your life
along the road of fate,
I found the garden of your heart
and I swung up on the gate.
Gazing at the daisies
and the tiny springtime shoots,
I trudged in through the flowerbed
in my shiny size-nine boots.
I picked the only rose I saw
and dropped the petals to the floor,
then carved my name into a tree
and did not take my trash with me
as I left, content, over the fence,
with a souvenir bouquet -
and promised soon I'd come again
as I went on my way...

TO DO (OR FIRST WORLD PROBLEMS)

Forgive me my mental distraction.
I'm just not really feeling that fun -
perhaps it's an overreaction
but there's so many things to get done!
There is trimming toenails and there's writing emails
and there's reading the things that come in;
there is sorting my music collection
and the cleaning routine of my skin.

There's weeding, and reading, and sleeping and snacking,
and presents for people to get;
there's putting out bins on the pavement,
and the keeping alive of my pet.
There's the making of beds and the baking of bread,
and there's billions of bills I must pay,
and there's peeing, and the posting of letters,
and planning my next trip away...
There's doctors and dentists and haircuts,
and hobbies and learning a trade;
there's Christmas and such
and there's keeping in touch
and there's millions of art to be made!

There's walking and working and wanking and washing,
and waiting in line for a bus,
there's the drinking of tea, and there's family to see,
and enormous amounts to discuss.
There's banking and bathing and shopping and shaving,
and just getting there in the car,
there's fighting for freedom and justice!
And admin. And learning guitar.
There is making phone calls, and repainting my walls,

and hearing the birds as they sing,
and there's learning it's best to be honest,
and then being with all that it brings.

There's massage, yoga, meditation, movies,
theatre and TV;
there's fixing and maintaining stuff,
and then there's tax and MOT.
There's relating and dating, and do-it-yourself,
and there's mouths to repeatedly feed,
and blogging and jogging and getting to bed,
and the helping of all those in need.
There's weddings, parties, procreation,
cleaning up and keeping fit,
and make-up and meals out and meetings,
and politically giving a shit.

There's the starting up of my own business,
and there's selling off all my old stuff;
all the hours where I share in a counsellor's chair
that I never quite feel I'm enough.
Oh, how is it true that there's so much to do?
I just don't get a window to think -
this culture is crazy (or maybe I'm lazy?)
but my lists they just don't seem to shrink...

I just don't comprehend
how my colleagues and friends
can all manage their families and homes
with the standards they keep
and still eight hours' sleep
and the Facebook account on their phones.

So when I'm poorly dressed
and my place is a mess,
understand that I'm doing my best;
I've really not meant
to be quite so absent.
I will just have to cancel my rest...
No, I don't want the sack.
Yes, I will call you back.
Yes, I would like to see you again.
But this weekend is full,
and it all is until
I've succeeded to empty my brain.

But next month there just might be a morning
between Torquay and Totnes somewhere.
(But if we book it must come with a warning
that it's also reserved for self-care...)

SLIDING

PRIORITIES

The first things to be sacrificed,
when I am under stress,
are my sentiment
and hoovering
(which both result in mess).

RESENTFULLY YOURS

I pause before I ring you,
hold back things I want to say,
'cause my obvious besotment
gives a bit too much away.
I'm embarrassed I want to impress you.
I want You to be out of control,
to tell me you're helpless without me
and obsessed with me, body and soul.
I want to retain my composure
as aloof, unavailable me.
I want you to woo me and wish I was there,
while I stay elusive and free.
Oh, have needs so I can disdain them,
just stop taking this all day by day -
yes, this is the truthful discomfort I sought
but now I wish it would all go away!
Please tell me we're over,
so I can sleep at night.
Tell me that I'm not enough for you
and prove me right.
I work hard when we're apart
to wriggle from your spell,
but you're so bloody open and constant and nice
I'm stuck in loving hell.
Now, being pursued and withholding:
that's where it's at in my books,
but getting with someone I do like this much
is harder than it looks.

NO

Just because you meditate, and fix, and drive a van,
just because my mother asks me, 'Who's the nice young man?',
just because our eyes connect in every silent pause,
just because you like me - it doesn't mean I'm yours.

Just because I check my texts more often than I ought,
just because you found a way to stalk my waking thoughts,
just because our bodies brush together without cause,
just because you like me - it doesn't mean I'm yours.

Just because I want to call with details of my day,
just because I'm reassured by all the things you say,
just because my rebel body rises at your touch,
just because you like me - it doesn't mean that much.

Just because your neck beckons with safety for my tears,
just because your smile defies a reason for my fears,
just because I'm melting when your breath lands on my skin,
just because you like me - doesn't mean I'll let you in.

I'm not your type, I'm overweight,
we're bound to miscommunicate -
I'll wear you down, we'll disagree,
you're so much tidier than me;
you'll hate the way I do so much,
we will not resonate in touch -
this isn't real, it will not last;
love doesn't come simple and fast...

And just because I checked the mirror twice before you came,
just because I tried the sound of taking on your name,
just because I might have mouthed your name, alone in lust,
just because I like you - it doesn't mean I'll trust.

FREQUENT FREQUENCIES

I am mostly easy-listening, but every now and then
I tune my inner radio to Drama FM.

GOOD MORNING

Sometimes I'm a monster,
and sometimes I am me;
I never know from day to day
which one I'm going to be.

LET THEM EAT...

I know I shouldn't snack so much
and chew food as I'm walking down the street.
I know that I should use a plate,
and sit down at a table when I eat.
I know I ought to learn to cook
and make sure I have hot food every day.
I know that I should clean up in the kitchen,
and should always do my dishes right away.

I should eat less, and take smaller spoons,
and contemplate the miles in every bite.
I should stop before I'm full,
and not eat anything past six o'clock at night.
I should remember to be grateful
and to speak a prayer of thanks at every meal.
I should leave something on my plate
to be a symbol of how satisfied I feel.

I should cut out sugar, chocolate, coffee,
cookies, cake and sweets,
and yeast, and fat, and white bread,
dairy, drinking and red meat,
and gluten, foreign fruit, and non-fair trade, and GMO.
I should be counting carbs and calories,
and keep cholesterol low.
I should not store my food in plastic,
should not microwave or fry;
I should not turn to food for comfort when I really need to cry.
I should try harder with my manners
while I'm entertaining guests.
I should brush my teeth when I am done,
    and then walk while I digest.

I know I should have five a day,
and soak and sprout and juice, and eat it raw.
I know I should take vitamins,
and flush and cleanse and detox till I'm pure.
I know I should shop locally,
and grow my own organic fruit and veg.
I know I should buy bulk supplies,
and go and pick my salads from the hedge.

I should always read ingredients
and scorn the things with too much packaging.
I should be drinking lots more water, sure it's filtered,
mineral or from a spring.
I should keep my pH alkaline
and never mix my starch up with protein.
I should be careful to have healthy oils,
and watch out for this dampness in my spleen.

I should ferment stinky things in jars and buckets full of slime.
I should boil up bones and offal like they did in ancient times.
I should add in algae, kale and greens,
and chia seeds, and sprouted beans,
and turmeric and manuka, and apple cider vinegar,
and pollen, gojis, hemp and clay, and oil-pulling twice a day,
and maca, flax and superfoods; I should not ever be so rude
as to turn my host down and refuse!

I know I should chew every bite one hundred times
and deeply contemplate.
I know that I should eat the fruit
before the other things upon my plate.
I know I should refuse dessert
and starve out my candida till it dies.

I know that I would eat right
for my ayurvedic blood type to be wise...

I should wash and cut my vegetables according to their chi.
I should cleanse my plate with reiki to adjust the energy.
I should start my day with lemon juice, and not a cup of tea.
I should never drink at mealtimes
(but I should drink my own wee).

I should not diet or miss mealtimes,
or be overly obsessed.
I should not have shame or guilt round food,
or eat while I'm stressed.
I should not believe an expert knows my body more than me.
I should not indulge in hang-ups;
food should always be carefree.
I should speed up with this menu,
'cause I'm taking far too long
and my date is looking worried
that there might be something wrong.
I should not 'should', should not 'ought to',
should not 'should not', should not take
all these guilty thoughts as gospel
- perhaps I'll shut them up with cake?

COLLIDING

I'M SUCH AN OXYMORON SOMETIMES

FUCK OFF!
I'm scared, hold me...
Come here - go away!
I love you - I hate you - everything's fine,
just tell me that I'm okay...?
Don't leave me, I'll be lonely,
I need you - set me free!
I'm doing fine all by myself,
just what do you want from me?
Just save me, don't blame me, don't ask why I cry,
I'm angry and hurt and I'm brave, and I'm shy.
Give me leave to be present and leave to be gone;
Step in when I'm falling - stay out when I'm strong.

Don't come too close, it's all too much,
S-l-o-w d-o-w-n - IT'S NOT ENOUGH!
marry me - let me go - give me some time,
treat me gently - I'm tough.
Don't worry - I'm seething - I never get mad.
DO. It. NOW. I can wait...
I'll never make it, I'm not gonna try.
Tell me again why I'm great...?
Don't do that - I love you just as you are.
I don't want you with me (but don't go too far).
I believe in commitment. And in changing my mind.
I won't be a leader, or follow behind.

Whatever it is, I can do it.
I succeed, and achieve, and survive.
But I'm hopeless and lonely and frightened and small,
and I need you to help me get by.
I'm wiser and better and perfect.

I'm hungry - I want to be thin.
I need challenge, and safety and comfort, and risk;
it just isn't fair. I give in.
I grant you your freedom - just don't look around.
Don't offer to help me, but don't let me drown!
Do just what you want to, but notice I'm upset,
don't pet me, accept me, that's all that you get.

I'm lost but don't show it, I'm hurt but won't say,
I doubt my own words - but I'll fight anyway.
Get out of my space! but just make sure you call?
Don't bug me, just love me.
...I miss you, that's all.

KNIGHT WITH THE DOUBLE-EDGED SWORD

I remember a time when things were calmer,
without this complicated drama,
without my knight in shining armour;
I just believed
in ME.

I had a rose garden of autonomy.
It was eeeeeasy;
there was no fairytale,
no female v. male conspiracy,
no one- or three- or five-year plan,
no angry-man stuff,
no mess.
NO STRESS.
(And, yeah, I guess no sex either - but it was worth it.)

Things aren't the same since you came.
Now I've got the whole deal:
the feelings,
the frustration,
the ever-endless negotiation...
the waiting...

I remember a time when I could choose something and just do it,
get my head down and go through it.
Snacking,
slacking,
staying up late.
(Ok, not all of it was that great, but I could do it
ON MY OWN.)

Now what have I got?

Well, I suppose, a flat, food, a phone,
someone to hold me at night,
it is quite nice when we don't fight
and, yeah, I guess you are right sometimes
about how things should be.

I remember a time when I was
QUEEN OF THE WORLD,
didn't need nothing from no one,
I could take the whole damn show on,
and now I'm just somebody's girl.

Well.

Don't tell.

But it's okay.

I guess I'll stay.

(For now.)

If we don't row and I get my way.

Yeah - maybe it's your lucky day

this time...

PHONE CALL

It's only been two
hours since you
left and I've eaten too many cookies, and, yes,
my tummy aches and I feel sick
(and I've realised I'm a complete bitch)
and I'm feeling guilty and selfish and sad
'cause I never said sorry, though I wish that I had,
and I tried to disguise what you knew all along,
that I lied when I told you that nothing was wrong.
I took you for granted, and wasted our time,
and it ruined a visit that would have been fine.
After all of that time I was wishing you'd go,
as soon as you did I felt very alone,
and now it's gone for good I see exactly what was there
and I regret that it seemed like I really didn't care
and I'm sorry I involved you, but I'm learning to be real -
and I can't ask for forgiveness, but I wonder how you feel...
It was insulting and depressing that you had to keep on guessing,
and these words don't do justice to the message I'm expressing,
and I know that I was awful, and I wish it wasn't true,
and so that's why I'm calling up right now.
um. "How are you?"

COPING

SCIENCE-FICTION FANTASY

If you want to wake up from the matrix,
instead of watching it all on repeat,
you gotta shake off your comfy delusions
and stand up on your unsteady feet.
You gotta get up off the sofa
before you're too long in the tooth -
and risk representing some realness
in the face of the butt-ugly truth.
Gotta take that red pill of awareness
despite you not liking your finds,
(and remember that all of those bullets
are only a trick of the mind...).

To graduate as a wizard from Hogwarts
or the imminent castle of Roke,
you gotta exchange your true name with the doorman
and let go of the mirrors and smokes.
You gotta keep peace with an elder,
and sleep in a niche in the wall,
and keep your ear out for the owls
who will summon you there with their call...
You gotta stoop to the lowliest questions,
and then run at full pelt at the bricks,
and not get distracted by Darkness
or the pride in your fanciful tricks.

But
to stay in the play as my partner,
there are far fewer hoops to jump through;
just accept that I'm not really there yet -
and admit it that neither are you.
But commit to the thrill of still trying

and keep sending our grades in to Roke,
then together we'll run through invisible walls
in the hope of our own staff and cloak.
And we'll neck every red pill that crosses our path
and be closer to truth with each one,
as two broken humans who'll never be fixed
but are bonded by want of a wand...

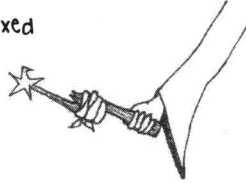

UPSIDE

When a lover really likes you
more than you like them
it sucks.
(But better that than finding
they were just collecting fucks.)

IRRATIONAL PASSION

I've given everything for love.
I've been wrecked upon its shore.
I have sacrificed my sanity,
then got up and given more.

BAD DAY

Poetry
seems to be
the only thing
I've going for me.

I DECLINE

Some people like climbing up mountains;
they hike every hillside that's there.
They will scrabble up slopes, with the highest of hopes,
of the wind and the view and the air.
But me - I like forests and valleys;
I like to stay close to the ground.
I'm not in this game for the conquest -
I always prefer to go down.

MOPING

SEEMING UNSEEN

Autonomous anonymous;
I'm just a person on a bus,
I'm just a stranger that you passed,
a memory that will not last,
a background accident-component
captive in your photo moment,
a silent watcher as you fight
to waste more breath on being right.
I'm there and gone, in drifts of smoke,
bite any hand that comes to stroke;
twisting out, dissolving fast,
so soon an echo in your past.
I choose where I want to go.
I'm difficult to get to know.
I brush against you - not for long -
to taste a dream I might belong...

ALTARED

mud, blood, sick, sore, face-down on the forest floor.
Open wide and fallen hard, cobwebs and mirror shards.
Dew-damp, wings torn, ashes in a thunderstorm;
leaves, hair, skin, soil, winding vines and mind uncoiled.
Scales and silk and horns and breath;
petals, weapons, salt and death.

Egg, belly, seed, fruit; mighty branches, mighty roots.
Flesh and flame and wind-blown stone,
loom and drum and bowl of bone.
Fur and fang and tail and claw,
a shriek, a sob, the distant roar.
Tears and breasts and moss and bark;
sweetly singing in the dark.

LOW POINT

I am Cundrie, I'm Ragnell,
I'm the tolling of the bell,
I'm all that's vile beneath the cloak,
I'm the wailing that you choke.
Eyes that rot to see disgrace;
I'm all that you don't want to face,
your innards dripping in full view,
the silent twisted part of you.
I am crawling with disgust,
ugly in my awful lust,
I'm a rancid staring beast,
the flies upon the hag-spoiled feast.
I am madness, I am sin,
I'm all the pain you lock within,
I'm contagious raw decay,
sick-flecked spittle on display.
I'm your failure in plain sight,
the hollow aching in the night,
the hated crone who comes to call;
the horror that's inside us all.

THE FALL

Autumn arriving in straight after Spring
is one of existence's most tragedous things.

HOPING

THE SKIN I WAS IN

Naked in the desert I have rolled down dunes,
I've spent evenings in the treetops singing loudly to the moon,
I've been lost upon the water in a sinking fishing boat,
and I have heard the earth's disgruntlement
through her volcano throat.
I've been with semi-naked ladies
bathed in dollars and champagne,
I've seen men bleeding from the needle-holes
that couldn't find a vein,
I've played with nitroglycerine, and I've jumped out of the sky,
and I made the 999 call for my love who tried to die.
I have chained myself in front of trucks,
and climbed an office block,
I've been up inside the bell tower with the striking of a clock,
I've seen some bodies buried, and I've seen some babies born,
and I've been photoed, filmed and painted
in the crazy things I've worn.

So, St Peter, if I lose a game to the cunning hand of fate,
I'll gather those things up to me, and meet you at the gate
with a knapsack full to bursting with my evidence of deeds:
pictures, poems, rings and letters, bells and bones and seeds.
But before you check the holy scroll and ask me for my name,
I might cast the contents at your feet and set them all aflame...
It would scorch my cheeks to feel the heat
of a thousand burning glories,
and I'd cry to see the embers die,
of my half-remembered stories.

But then, silent by the ashes, I might sit and wait, alone.
Until a lengthy time had gone - and a single rose had grown.
And I'd wear that rose in my lapel, to the wake of she who died;
then I'd turn towards the pearly doors, and make my way inside...

SOMETHING ABOUT A CAMEL
AND A NEEDLE

If I died and met St Peter, and he asked me what I'd done,
I'd say, 'I'll tell you gladly, I've not done badly;
I've have a lot of fun...
I'm not too old and all told
I've lived through quite momentous things.
My life was stuffed, but now I'm snuffed
I want my harp and wings.'
St Peter would say, 'OK, that's a start,
I can see you're not full of regret,
but to get through these gates isn't easy, my friend,
and you've not earned the wristband just yet.
What deems you so deserving, to be saved from all your sin?
'Cause if your name isn't on this list - you are so not coming in...'

So I'd speak of yarns from my misspent years
(with accumulated pride),
whilst peeping through the pearly gates to dearly pass inside...
a reputation résumé, in a reel of anecdotes:
every double-ended candle, every hoarded cause to gloat,
each attendance to perfection, each insistent victory,
when - by way of a correction - good ol' Pete would say to me,
'Really? Well, you're clearly a lady who's loved life
and lived it whatever the deal,
but you haven't said much about how you were touched,
or how anything caused you to feel...'

So I'd list all those who liked me, because I tried so hard.
And I'd tell him of my travels: every brave exotic yard.
I'd list all the awards and the trophies I'd won,
and all of the dangerous tough things I'd done,
until, awaiting my fate at the gates,

I might pause - and St Peter would suffer no more.
He'd say, 'Princess, it's tragic you've passed on,
but really I'm not very sure
what bearing these things have on halos and wings,
and if I should draw back this bolt.
Perhaps I can help you to open your heart?
Don't worry, it's nobody's fault...

'Did you ever tend a tiny seed with care and watch it grow?
Did you give away a precious thing, while hurting to let go?
Did you give your time to be with those who simply needed care?
Have you sat long beside the ashes,
till your shadow met you there?

'Did you stop to see a flower uncurl and slowly greet the day?
Then did you mourn to see such beauty in remembrance of decay?
Did you earn your limp with madness
from the hollow tree of grief?
Have you ever been left tearful at the falling of a leaf?

'Did you give the earth your hunger?
Did you kneel to greet the sun?
Did you walk a queen among the queens,
and always bless the young?
Did you ever work without reward, in service never seen?
Did you make a bed of roots and hay, and give way to routine?

'Did you show up as your ugly twin and let the love inside?
Did you stop your car to move the dead
and dying from the roadside?
Were you grateful? Were you sorry? Did you truly taste and see?
Have you let go of the shore you know?
If so, then you can come inside, with me...'

I'd say, 'I'm sorry I've been busy, Pete,
in all my years of late,
stocking up on noble deeds to prove that I am great.
I didn't sit, or breathe, or wait, or watch a changing sky...
perhaps I could go down again to have another try?
And this time I'd be humble,
and this time I'd be real,
and this time I'd show everyone just how I really feel!
I'd say all the things I left unsaid; I hope it's not too late.
So stuff your wristband up your dress,
and screw your pearly gates.'

SHAMEAWAY

Are you AFFLICTED by your weakness?
Are you ADDICTED to your thoughts?
Are you SICK of oversharing?
Do you CONCEDE more than you ought?
Have you TRIED eye contact lately?
Do you HIDE most of the time?
Are you TERRIFIED of people?
Then you'll NEED our new hotline.
Are you OPPRESSED by your behaviour?
Well, today's your lucky day,
Because now there is a saviour;
Dump your meds for SHAMEAWAY!

Just one tablet turns the tables,
Flips unacceptance into pride.
Now you can walk the streets a monster.
melt the masks to your inside.

Parade your naked deformation
In brash defiance of the norm.
Send them scurrying for safety
With the abomination of your form.

Ask too many stupid questions.
make it plain that you don't know.
Bear no regard to your rejection.
Rudely interrupt the flow.

Point at all avoided elephants.
Let rip with inappropriate retorts.
Scoff the multipack of Frazzles
And wash 'em back with swigs of port.

Beg for scraps of affirmation.
Weep unapologetically at feet.
Say goodbye to chores and hygiene.
Marinate in filthy sheets.

Walk away from every dullard.
Snarl each time you catch a glance.
Gorge on chips and chocolate fingers.
Let your shadow have its chance.

Loudly boast about your foibles.
Seek thou not success or fame.
No more striving for inclusion.
Epic failure is yours to claim.

Wear your weirdo on the outside.
See your beliefs reborn anew.
Let your inner toddler dress you.
SHAMEAWAY for me and you.

(New Shameaway and Shameaway Spray
For a limited time only, so buy today!)

Embrace a fearless freedom at your very fingertips.
Fully live with boundless liberation on your lips.
Don't be sorry, don't be careful, don't be charming, don't be nice.
Special offer SHAMEAWAY is cheap at twice the price!

SORRY

I am not uncomplicated. I'm not always well behaved.
I'm not someone who is always fine;
I've not come though unscathed.
I am not a model daughter. I am not a perfect host.
I am not one who can be categorised as easily as most.
I'm not a Persian or Parisian, a surfer or cyclist;
I'm not someone spontaneous who can live without a list.
I am no high income earner; I'm not an owner of a home;
I'm not a concert concertinist or a maestro on the bones.
I'm no top-deck executive or sassy CEO;
I'm not someone who risks the truth in every status quo.
I'm not a lady with a baby. I'm not a lady with a man.
I'm not a lady with expensive haircuts, make-up and a tan.
I'm not a hairless high-heeled hottie or a sanguine socialite;
I'm no bikini-bodied blonde with birdlike appetite.
I am not dressed up by Ann Summers,
nor am I styled by Saint Laurent.
I'm not one who feels normal through
the Debenhams make-up run.
I'm not a barefoot gypsy girl, a fairy or an elf.
I just might be in the next life,
but right now - I'm something else.

RAVEN IMAGE

Y'know Aesop's
fables, when the old fox
turned the tables on
the crow with the cheese?
It was sitting high in the treetops
and the sly fox said,
'Please!
Why don't you sing for me?
Your melodies are THE most beautiful thing I've ever heard.'
And the feathered wings of the bird puffed up,
and he coughed, and as he opened his jaw to caw
he dropped his precious snack and SNAP!
He saw it swallowed by the fat fox, and that was that.

That story's haunted me
since primary school assembly
in 1988, and lately
I've come to see that crow as me.
Aloof in my tree, clinging desperately
to some prize jeopardised by compliments!
And in defence I keep my beak closed tight
and pray my weakness might not
let my heart slip
away into the grip of whoever passes by
casting eyes in my direction.

Praise be denied;
for self-protection I deride every mention that might incite pride
(even though inside this bird there may be a song
that longs to be heard...).
I suspect the objective of any kind words.

No, flattery will not get the better of me.
I sing for none;
no generous tongue can coax my bounty free.
This humility intact, though folks may try hard
I've not cracked;
I'm on guard at my perch,
alone and alert,
'cause I've learned to spurn what I yearn to believe.
And what the tale from my ailing headmaster achieved,
what that story did for me, was teach me... suspicion;
to meet the sweet-talkers and piss on their mission,
to obtain my cheese with eulogies.

School taught I ought not to be foolish or vain,
to trust only injustice, maintain my disdain for lip service,
to sneer at the idea that I could be good,
and to keep all my cheese to myself, as I should.

So why not, foxes? Let's get out of our boxes...
I'll sing, and you can applaud, unrewarded,
the flaws I swore I'd never fall for exposing.
And indeed, I can enjoy your acclaim without pain,
and dare to share this wealth that I've gained
without need to be wary of stealth or deceit -
'cause down on the ground we can all have a piece.
Y'know, that tree was lonely, and it's a relief
to be here without fearing the fate of my snack - 'cause
if you're quick with the pickle I'll go get the crackers
and we can dine at a table with sunshine above,
and make our own fable - with wine and with love.

CLIMBING

INSPIRED BY RYALLS PARK
POETRY POSSE '17

So you think you're crazy?
So you think there's something wrong?
So you think you're out of tune with all the other songs?
So you think you're different?
So you think you're not enough?
So you think the world would end if we all knew your stuff?
So you think you're not important?
So you think you're not okay?
So you think you don't fit in, and you should hide away?
So you think this pain inside belongs to you alone?
So you think that something terrible would happen if it's shown?
So you think you're broken?
So you think you have cause for shame?
So you really think the other people in this room are sane?

Do you really?
Do you really?
Do you really?

Well,
don't you think I'm terrified?
That sometimes I want to die?
Don't you think a story lies inside each pair of eyes?
Don't you know you're whole with all your wounding and your fears?
Don't you think your wisdom might be gold dust for our ears?
And doesn't some deep part of you believe this isn't right?
Don't you long for stepping forwards, out into the light?
Don't you have a craving to be welcome, As You Are?
Don't you know we're all amazing, awkward and bizarre?
Don't you know we're all misshapen?
Don't you know that we're all weird?

Don't you know it might not be as lonely as you feared?
Don't you know that it's okay to feel dark, or hurt, or sad?
(And don't you think it's interesting to be a little mad?)
Don't you know you are unique and you still make perfect sense?
Don't you know what's normal is confusion, not pretence?
And don't you find it crazy that we all could be more true?
Don't you know you're wanted - as the real, imperfect you?
Don't you know we're all puzzle pieces laid out on a floor?
Don't you know... you do not have to worry any more?

OVER YOULOGY

She never got a proper job, she never had a home,
she loved and lost and loved and lost,
but she always lived alone.
She struggled with emotion, she learned so many things,
but she never had a lot to show for her multitude of strings.
She was loyal, brave and truthful; she tried and tried and tried,
but she never shook her smallness or her tendency to hide.
She believed in magic.
She thought the world was good.
There was much that she still wanted,
and she did the best she could.

FOR JEFF (AND EVERYONE EVER)

Dear Jeff,
you're best
at being you.
It's a job
that no one
else can do.
You're the only
one who can
bring through
for us
this unique man.

No one can live
the life you live,
no one can give
the hugs you give,
no one else
has got your smile,
no one else
has got your style.

Dear Jeff,
we need you
as you are:
bumps and bruises,
tender scars.
You're wild
and wise,
and joyful too,
which everyone can see
but you...

Comparison
can go to hell.
Just live your story,
do it well.
Centre stage
or out of sight,
just being Jeff's
exactly right.
No one can bring
the gifts you bring,
no one can sing
the song you sing,
your Jeffness is
a special thing -
you're Jeff!

Dear Jeff,
you're best
at being you.
If you
won't do it
then, hell, who?
It doesn't matter
what you're not;
just give it
everything
you've got.

No one else
can speak your heart,
no one else
can play your part.
No one has

your eyes, your brain,
no one else
will feel your pain.

Dear Jeff,
we need you
as you are,
humble man
or superstar...
Scholar,
lover, worker,
chief:
what's important's
underneath.
Equality
is in the soul;
you're already
perfect, whole.
There's nothing more
you must become,
there's always something
left undone.
No one translates
the world like you,
the one and only
Jefflike view,
So fuck
what other people do;
you're Jeff!

SHINING

I LIKE ME

I like being me - it means I can go out
without preening or plucking, or mucking about;
I don't have to check if my mascara's run,
or pick tiny pants from the crack of my bum.
I like being me - I don't have to look pretty
and be freezing in a tiny top the whole night in the city.
You'll never see me struggle in my high heels up a street,
teetering discreetly, 'cause I got pity for my feet.

I like being me - I am fast in the bath;
I don't endure the custom of dilapidation rash.
Film stars, fads and fashions pass me by without a care,
I do not even own a brush for this fantastic hair.
I like being me - I don't fold clothes or iron.
You will never see me working with a collar and a tie on.
I get to wear big stomping boots and jump around, and fight,
and when I dance I do it without needing to look right.

I wear things with holes in, I don't need my socks to match.
I can see a pile of washing up and feel no need to act.
I can leave a bed unmade, and drop things on the floor;
I'm free from all compulsion to arrange them in a drawer.
My lifestyle choice is easy, I have time and money spare
(I must do other useless things instead, but I don't really care).
I get paid to play with poems, and have as much fun as I can.
I wouldn't swap the life I've got; I love being who I am.

REASONS TO BE CHEERFUL

I like the smash of glass
as it crashes on the bottom of the bottle bank.
I like to peel pictures that people have pressed,
to look at the patterns of glue that they left.
I'd like to make a scrapbook of cuttings that I find,
and paste them all in forwards to display what was behind.
I like to say the sounds of shapes,
and speak the words in licence plates.
I like Christmas-cracker novelties for their complete inanity, and
lost-pet posters as a showcase of humanity.
I like pouring olive oil, slowly from a spout,
and inspecting the reflections as the liquid trickles out.
I like to find things perfect places,
and fit them all in smaller spaces.
I like the patterns in puddles that come in foam-forming bubbles
and spirals of scum,
the large arms of fathers enfolding their charges
of children to cherish and hold.
I like to see steam swirl from tea until the cup goes cold.
I'd like to work as a post-office clerk,
and assert my stamp with vigour.
I like to use those sundae spoons
with handles that are bigger.
I love the efficient little cardboard pops
when I'm folding up the flaps of a pizza box.
I like the smell of coriander, and the funny shape of feet.
I like it when a bird-shaped shadow skims across the street.
I like to fill my hand with sand and slowly let it go.
I like to be the first to leave fresh footprints in the snow.

I always like riding more than arriving
when out anywhere for a drive. I like to firmly fix my fork in the
turf when I'm working outside.
I like the sight of bright sun on the ground
when the distance is darkened by threatening cloud.
I like to imagine I swim or I fly,
by dropping or diving when clifftops are high.
I like walloping bollards I pass in the street,
with slap from palm of my hand.
I like the lines left behind by the tide,
and the breaking of water on sand.
I love to see silhouettes of the trees,
when their branches are bare and they've lost all their leaves.
I like to slice with the sharpest of knives,
into onions that crunch when they cut.
I like to keep spaces small where I sleep,
with the doors closed and curtains all shut,
and I love it when autumn leaves land in the rain,
and print on the pavement the shape of their stain.
I like egg-shapes, and velvet, and silver, and shadows,
and children, and chocolate, and lying in meadows,
and abandoned umbrellas - broken by weather
and left in a skeletal wreck.
I like rainbows in eyelashes, bubbles and oil-splashes,
breath on the back of my neck.

AFFIRMATION SONG!

Chorus:
By the universe, I am held; I am fit and I am well.
I'm receptive to the infinite blessings and signs,
and consistently grateful in heart and in mind.

My beauty shines through me, I'm proud and I'm here,
I'm innocent always, feelings deep and clear.
I love myself more every day that I live,
I'm joyful in sharing everything I can give.

(Chorus)

I can build any vision, I create what I need.
I'm humble but certain, I inspire by my lead.
I am clean and courageous; I let people see
the truth of my power and my vulnerability.

(Chorus)

I'm as worthy as all those I judge and respect.
I'm vibrant, and open to flow and connect.
Absolute liberation, embodied with ease;
it feels good to me to take up space and act on energies!

(Chorus)

I am loved and supported, I chose intimacy.
I'm committed to care for the gifts given me.
I welcome the limits preserving my health.
I rest in abundant harmonious wealth.
I surrender, I find my centre, I trust and remember;
I already know. I sacrifice wisely, I discern the best option,
I make choices for my highest good,
and let go...

OWNING IT

BELIEVE THE BIRD

(after James Audubon, who said it first)

If the book says one thing
in its eternal inky words
and the blackbird sings another thing,
then please
believe the bird.

'Cause a monk one day
was trying to figure it all out
so he asked his master
what the world was all about
and the answer of the master
wasn't anything he said,
but it was taking off a single shoe
to put it on his head!

And if the book says one thing
in its eternal inky words
and the skylark sings another thing,
then please
believe the bird.

When two monks crossed the river bridge
to reach the other side,
said one, 'I wonder if this water's
deep as it is wide...'
Why his friend did not respond to this enquiry,
he was stumped,
until he turned around to realise the man already jumped.

'Cause if the book says one thing
in its eternal inky words

and the robin sings another thing,
then please
believe the bird.

There was a hungry begging monk
who sat upon the street,
who was given two whole loaves of bread
so he could finally eat,
but straight away he sold one
for a penny in his bowl -
and he went to buy some hyacinths
so that he could feed his soul.

'Cause if the book says one thing
in its eternal inky words
and the owl, it sings another thing,
then please
believe the bird.

IN MY DEFENCE

Yes, I know that oneness;
I know it very well.
It was me - before my birth -
and it awaits my death as well.
It's always been the truth of me,
I know it always will
(and it always is available
if I sit very still...).

But what use is there to arms and legs
if I don't push and swim,
and fight and love and taste things,
and express what I took in?
You may question why I'm busy,
why I run around so much,
but what's the purpose of a person
if not to play and learn and touch?

Experience and awareness
are my wealth while I'm on earth,
for this brief time in a body
between the doors of death and birth.
I love this crazy planet;
the pleasure and the pain.
I want to see and do it all,
before I'm one again.

SMALL PRINT

I'm gonna be quiet, complex, erratic.
A paradox-ymoron, idiosyncratic.
You'll see that I'm messy, moody, chaotic;
I do things the hard way - don't try and stop it.
I'm shy and unwilling, I hide and avoid,
you're gonna get triggered, upset and annoyed...

I'm self-destructive, full of excuses,
ambiguous, vague, evasive, elusive.
I'm inconsistent, contradictory, never content,
I'm keen on control - I rebel and dissent.
I'll resist definition, I won't be confined,
I reserve all the rights upon changing my mind.

I will not be configured, fixed or fast-tracked.
I will sit on the fence, defend and react.
I'll expect you to get what I think-but-don't-say.
Sometimes I like problems and I leave them that way.
I'm stubborn and stressy, I'll sulk and I'll blame,
I'll cry and disguise things, and cover my shame.

I'm gonna find fault, and I'll pine and I'll moan,
I'll hanker for freedom and time all alone.
I killed all the plants and the pets that I've had.
I'll withdraw into weakness whenever you're mad.
I'm confusing, I lose things, I leave stuff around.
I will not be worked out, boxed in, or pinned down.

I'll always be awkward, never straightforward,
I cling to the crap I've collected and hoarded.
I'll be proud and conceited and seething and sly,
all this (and more), which I'll mostly deny,
you're so brave and so trusting in wanting me near -
so thank you, my darling; now just / sign / here...

HYPERGRAPHIA

my name's Beryl, and I am an inkaholic.
I wrote this because
poetry's a product of it.

I'm a compulsive list-maker;
addicted to pen and paper,
I'm a rhyme-shaper, an abbreviator,
an I-can't-read-it-later note-taker...
a page-slave.
At home I wade through phone numbers with no names,
I've got ink in my veins.
my pupils are punctuation marks.

Just one more hit, I need this fix,
you'll frequently find me foraging for bits
in the recycling tray.
Encrypted script is my defence
so that no one clicks it's all nonsense,
coded with acronym, symbol and speed,
that no other person can possibly read -
I've a shorthand even I don't understand,
and hence... (what did that bit say?)

I'm a compulsive list-maker;
addicted to pen and paper,
I put pens in my hair
and then forget where they've gone.
(It's thanks to me that the ones in banks are all tied on.)
I'm a pen kleptomaniac,
collecting tiny paper scraps,
practising on napkins, or on packaging and ticket backs.
I always bring utensils,

I carry extra pencils,
I'd go mental if I didn't vent the sentences in here.
Got one drawing implement behind each ear.
I spend time reading signs and picking up fliers,
but it sees me through the winter 'cause I need to feed my fires.

I'm a compulsive list-maker;
addicted to pen and paper,
I'm a hand-scribbler, biro-nibbler,
noticeboard junky, small-ad flunky.
I'm a page-a-week organiser freak.
My fingers twitch in my sleep...
I've got jotters dotted all round my home
and cases of pencils placed by the phone
and next to the desk and under the bed,
and I still can't vent enough stuff to empty out my head...
but each line leads to a short-lived freedom.
(I rarely feel the need to read them.)

Once, I vowed not to write anything down
for ten days, whilst on retreat,
but I nearly went crazy just halfway through that week
and found myself, with a paper towel sheet
(this is true), locked in the loo,
with a decoction of coffee to dip my finger into...
and I wrote those notes in blissful reprise!
(I only wish they'd said something wise.
I'm just one giant mark-making exercise...)

I'm a compulsive list-maker,
addicted to pen and paper,
a rhyme-shaper, an abbreviator...
etc.

(...Is there someone I could see for diary dependency?)

BLOOMIN' HARD WORK

I'm difficult to get to know;
I think you should be warned.
You'd have to scale a greasy stalk
while gored by barb'rous thorns.

But beyond all my defences,
I am an open flower,
freely sweet with nectar
and surrendered in my power.

WOMANIFESTO

more space, less time.
more circle, less line.
Less tool, more hand.
Less money, more land.
more truth, less shame.
more heart, less brain.
more hearth, less screen.
Less sense, more dream.
Less shops, more sky.
more veg, less pie.
Less people, more place.
Less phone, more face.
more vest, less bra.
Less roof, more stars.
more boots, less heels.
more legs, less wheels.
more herbs, less meds.
Less bars, more bed.
Less nice, more wyrd.
Less wax, more beard.
Less table, more floor.
more less, less more.
more story, less chat.
Less dog, more cat.
more play, less stress.
more pants, less dress.
Less pants, more skin.
more out, less in.
more breath, more trees, more life, more wonder.
more drenched and howling in the thunder.
more touch, more bodies, more being, more bliss.
more art, more magic.
more me.
more this.

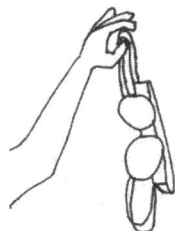

IN THE MOMENT

I'm not the me I used to be,
I'm not so bright and wild.
I'm not the me I used to be,
I'm much less of a child.
I'm not the me I used to be,
my hair is turning white.
I'm not the me I used to be
now stillness is alright.

ABOUT THE WORD/PLAY PROJECT

Poems written 'for the Ryalls Park poetry posse' are inspired by the participants of *Word/Play*: a pioneering arts-on-prescription project for people with mental health concerns, run through the NHS by Somerset arts charity Take Art.

Patients are encouraged to attend the creative workshop series by Health Coaches who work with their GP. A supportive, non-judgemental space enables them to connect and be heard while additionally learning to write and perform expressive or autobiographical poetry.

The sessions have been astounding in their rewards, making *Word/Play* tangibly effective as an intervention. The approach is not only fun and affirming, but has improved well-being through the reinforcement of coping strategies and social networks; transforming isolation and anxiety by enhancing confidence and self-esteem.

Beryl has so far been privileged to co-facilitate two series at Ryalls Park Medical Centre, tracking shifts from states of introversion towards a candid sharing and playful camaraderie. She has seen some incredible participants step into their talent and blossom beyond the challenges of mental health, through this application of introspection, poetic tools, and dramatic spoken word.

Take Art hope to continue to grow the *Word/Play* method of Performance Poetry on Prescription (and other social-prescribing partnerships between the health, social care and Arts sectors), in order to reduce costs, impact levels of use, and avert dependency for care services.

A short film about *Word/Play* has been produced to promote the project's impact to the health and social care sectors:
To see the film or for more information please visit
www.takeart.org/word-play